GW00778354

Christianity, Islam
and
British Politics
ed C Cleall

A lecture given at the
Campaign for UK Conservatism Conference on
CONSERVATISM, EUROPE, AND THE FUTURE OF
THE CONSERVATIVE PARTY
Oxford Brookes University
Saturday, 26 November 2005

With Appendices
on
Islamic issues

Dr Alan C Clifford

Charenton Reformed Publishing

© Alan C Clifford 2006

First published in Great Britain 2006
by Charenton Reformed Publishing
www.geocities.com/nrchurch

Typeset in Sabon

British Library Cataloguing in Publication Data.
A catalogue record for this book is available from the British Librar

ISBN 0 9526716 9 7

Cover concept:
the Author, executed by Barkers Print & Design Ltd
The *upper* symbols represent our Protestant constitutional monarch
and parliamentary liberal democracy, both reflecting our national
Christian heritage.

The *lower* symbols represent all that threatens this heritage:
(left to right) Roman Catholicism, Nazi-style racism, global Islam ar
atheistic secularism/communism.

Rear cover logo:
Charenton Reformed Publishing and Norwich Reformed Church

Expressing a vision for a new English Reformed Church, the
Huguenot Cross (a symbol of the Reformed Faith) on the Cross of
George symbolises the true Reformed Faith in England.

Dedicated to the Memory
of the Children of Beslan
murdered by Islamic terrorists
on 3 September 2004
and
the three Indonesian girls
beheaded by Islamic militants
on 29 October 2005

"It would be better for him if a millstone were hung around his neck,
and he were thrown into the sea, than that he should offend
one of these little ones."

JESUS CHRIST
(Luke 17: 2)

Thought:

A religion whose activists can target children
must be inexpressibly evil.

THE ORIGINAL CONFERENCE DETAILS

The Campaign For the United Kingdom Conservatism
Individual-Family-Community-Nation-Rule of Law-Personal Capital
www.ukconservatism.freeuk.com
Unit B, West View Terrace, St Omers Road, Gateshead NE11 9EL

CONFERENCE, OXFORD BROOKES UNIVERSITY, OXFORD
Saturday 26th November 2005

"CONSERVATISM, EUROPE AND THE FUTURE OF THE CONSERVATIVE PARTY"

SPEAKERS

Chairman: Mr Rodney Atkinson

Rt Hon The Lord Tebbit, Former Chairman of the Conservative Party
Subject: *The Future of Conservative Party*

Gerald Howarth MP, Shadow Defence Minister
Subject: *Is EU Procurement policy a threat to UK Defence?*

Tim Congdon CBE, Economist & Former member of the Treasury Panel
Subject: *The Euro and EU political integration*

Revd Dr Alan Clifford, Pastor, Norwich Reformed Church
Subject: *Islam, Christianity and British Politics*

Beat Kaufmann, Head of Economics Section, Swiss Embassy London
Subject: *EFTA as an Alternative - the Swiss experience of the EFTA and the EU*

Lynn Riley, Co Founder, British Declaration of Independence
Subject: *Asserting the Sovereignity of the British people*

CONTENTS

PRAYER

While this is a political conference, and not a church service, I am a pastor rather than a politician. I invite you, therefore, to join me in prayer, using the petition for fortitude of Bishop Nicholas Ridley martyred for the cause of Christ in England here at Oxford 450 years ago

O HEAVENLY Father, the Father of all wisdom, understanding and true strength, we beseech Thee look mercifully upon Thy servants, and send Thy Holy Spirit into our hearts, that, when we must join to fight in the field for the glory of Thy Holy Name, we, being strengthened with the defence of Thy right hand, may manfully stand in the confession of Thy faith and of Thy truth, and continue in the same unto the end of our lives; through Jesus Christ our Lord. Amen.

Christianity, Islam and British Politics

I
INTRODUCTION

A glut of highly-significant secular and religious autumn anniversaries provides a stimulating context for my subject. Using more broadly the now-universal convention of identifying momentous events like New York's 9/11, Madrid's 3/11 and London's 7/7, I cite, first, some famous *secular* examples from more distant history.

First, we may recall 10/14, the Battle of Hastings, the last of four major invasions of the British Isles in a millennium by "Europeans" – 1066 and all that, of course! Then, more positively in this bicentenary year, there's 10/21, when "Europe" was on the receiving end of The Lord Nelson's decisive broadsides at the Battle of Trafalgar in 1805. Not till 1940 was this country seriously threatened again by a foreign power.

I pass by 10/25 in 1415. Agincourt, Henry V, and the savage nationalism of the Hundred Years' War, warrant national shame rather than pride. Indeed, driven by the power-hungry Plantagenets, the whole era has something of an "Iraq War" whiff about it! Another noted 10/25 was, of course, the distant Crimean Battle of Balaclava in 1854. Inglorious for the British High Command, the heroism of "the six hundred" is justly celebrated. Stepping into November, and closer to home, we rightly remember annually the enormously costly sacrifice represented by 11/11: the Armistice of 1918, when the four-year horror of the First World War came to an end.

Turning to *religious* anniversaries of great national significance, 10/16 should be recalled, especially in this University City of Oxford. Indeed, looking back 450 years to the Protestant Reformation, both Oxford and the Nation should honour (among nearly three hundred others in the reign of Bloody Mary) the heroic martyrdom of two bishops of the

Reformed Church of England: Hugh Latimer and Nicholas Ridley, in 1555. William Shakespeare never bettered Latimer's words spoken to Ridley shortly before they were both burned at the stake:

BE OF GOOD COMFORT, MASTER RIDLEY, AND PLAY THE MAN; WE SHALL THIS DAY LIGHT SUCH A CANDLE, BY GOD'S GRACE, IN ENGLAND, AS I TRUST SHALL NEVER BE PUT OUT.

Central to the Continental Reformation struggle, the French tragedy of 10/17 – representing an era of persecution lasting three centuries – had a definitely British impact too. The Revocation of the Edict of Nantes by King Louis XIV in 1685 sent Huguenot refugees all over Europe and beyond. To the severe detriment of France – a loss she suffers to this day – the French Reformed Protestants not only reinforced the Protestant ethos of this country. Their economic, technological, cultural and military expertise made them welcome immigrants indeed.

October ends with 10/31: the anniversary of Martin Luther's protest against Roman Catholic superstition, idolatry, corruption and tyranny in 1517; a German explosion which brought light and eventual liberty to much of Europe including Great Britain. Surely, without Luther, Latimer and Ridley would never have lit the candle of pure Christian truth in England.

Last, I cite an event with decidedly secular *and* sacred significance – the Gunpowder Plot. Indeed, the wonderful deliverance of 11/5 should *never* "be forgot", especially in this quatercentenary year. Luther's liberating work of the previous century might have been undone in a flash on that awesome day in 1605, had the Vatican's Jesuit-inspired terrorists succeeded.

In distinguishing between two categories of events, I am not assuming that all the apparently secular examples are without a religious dimension. The Gunpowder Plot is not alone in this respect – let us remember that The Pope blessed William the Conqueror's invasion of England. The same may be said of the first and second World Wars whose prehistory stretches back to the seventeenth century if not earlier.

Yet, in these "PC" times, the BBC provided us with a politically-correctly perverse history of the Gunpowder Plot in the run-up to this year's Guy Fawkes. The spin was predictable. To argue that we must avoid excluding groups from society on religious grounds or suffer the consequences is both naïve and dangerous. The simple fact is that the Roman Catholic conspirators of 1605 were enemies of the State professing allegiance to a hostile foreign power (both religious and political) which had excommunicated H M Queen Elizabeth I; given *carte blanche* to her would-be assassins, and backed the Spanish Armada in 1588. If the fate of the Vatican terrorists of 11/5 was gruesome over-kill, a nation thus threatened cannot afford to be lax over security.

In today's political terms, an otherwise liberal democracy cannot tolerate those who abuse its liberality by violence. Such a threat was not lost on the framers of *The Bill of Rights* (1689) and *The Act of Settlement* (1701). In short, it was reasonably argued that a Roman Catholic, Pope-serving monarch is a threat to the political as well as the religious liberties of a free people. In that the papal agenda continued unchanged, was not the 1829 *Catholic Emancipation Act* naïve and premature? Did our legislators imagine that the threat had passed forever?

When the Roman Catholic hierarchy was restored in 1850, Cardinal Wiseman resorted to Rome's usual rhetoric, declaring to his clergy, "It is good for us, reverend brothers, to be here in England. . . . It is for us to subjugate and subdue, to conquer and to rule, an imperial race. We have to do with a will which reigns throughout the world, as the will of old Rome reigned once; and it is for us to bend or break that will, which nations and kingdoms have found invincible and inflexible. Were [Protestant] heresy conquered in England, it would be conquered throughout the world" (R F Horton, *Shall Rome Reconquer England?* (1910), pp. 75-6).

In 1874, Cardinal Manning's rhetoric became more menacing: "There is one solution to the difficulty if England will not bow to The Pope, and that is the terrible scourge of a Continental war: a war which will exceed any of the horrors of the first Empire. And it is my firm conviction that, despite of all obstacles, The Vicar of Christ will be put again in his own rightful place. But that day will not come till his adversaries have crushed themselves with mutual destruction".

To cut a long story very short, *via* Vatican [pro-Nazi] intrigue during two wars, and the rise of the European Union (see the French Catholic historian Edmond Paris's *The Vatican Against Europe*), Rome's anti-British agenda has never changed. So, "Remember, remember, the Fifth of November!" – and set the UK free from the EU as soon as possible; preferably, before Turkey becomes a member!

Why do I mention all this? For those who dismiss all I've stated as jingoism, I hope they have detected a healthy Christian internationalism in my sketch of events. More than that – a decidedly *Protestant* Christian internationalism, unmoved as I am by Pope Benedict XVI's haughtily antichristian denial that Protestants have a valid churchmanship, ministry and sacraments (he is wrong, of course, as John Calvin would strongly remind us). Indeed, for some of the best features of British culture, we owe a great debt to the Protestants of Germany and France, not to forget the Netherlands (especially, in 1688, to William of Orange and "the Glorious Revolution").

Accordingly, as a *Christian* English patriot, I endorse the noble words of First World War, Norfolk heroine Edith Cavell: "Patriotism is not enough". I am reminded of Dr Johnson's well-known observation: "Patriotism is the last refuge of a scoundrel". In short, purest patriotism needs purest Christianity. Invoking the highly-appropriate motto of Oxford University "*Dominus illuminatio mea*" – "The Lord is my Light" (from *Psalm 27: 1;* Vulgate, *Psalm 26: 1*), it is the Light of God in Christ, Jesus "the Light of the world" (*John 8: 12*) Whom we need, as individuals and as a nation.

Hence, it is my thesis that Latimer and Ridley's "candle" represents all that is best and noblest in British culture – a heritage progressively betrayed by the secular establishment, undermined by a Vatican-inspired European ecumenism, and now threatened by Islam.

2
CRISIS

While it is vital to remember all this history, the threat of Islam is but the latest assault on the hard-won Christian-based cultural, political and social values of the United Kingdom. In the wider Western context, some are speaking in terms of a "clash of civilizations". Compared with our modern misty-eyed secularists, Sir Winston Churchill's view of Islam – written in 1899 when he was twenty-five – needs little amendment in 2005:

How dreadful are the curses which [Islam] lays on its votaries! Besides the fanatical frenzy, which is as dangerous in a man as hydrophobia in a dog, there is this fearful fatalistic apathy. The effects are apparent in many countries. Improvident habits, slovenly systems of agriculture, sluggish methods of commerce, and insecurity of property exist wherever the followers of the Prophet rule or live. A degraded sensualism deprives this life of its grace and refinement; the next, of its dignity and sanctity.

The fact that, in [Islamic] law, every woman must belong to some man as his absolute property (either as a child, a wife, or a concubine) must delay the final extinction of slavery till the faith of Islam has ceased to be a great power amoung men. Individual Muslims may show splendid qualities; thousands become the brave and loyal soldiers of The Queen; all know how to die: but the influence of the religion paralyses the social development of those who follow it

No stronger retrograde force exists in the world. Far from being moribund, [Islam] is a militant and proselytizing faith. It has already spread throughout Central Africa, raising fearless warriors at every step; and, were it not that Christianity is sheltered in the strong arms of science – the science against which it had vainly struggled, – the civilization of modern Europe might fall, as fell the civilization of ancient Rome" (*The River War* (1899), ii. 248-50).

As a not-irrelevant digression, one amendment at least is necessary. Even as he was writing, science had become increasingly hostile to Christianity since the publication of Darwin's *Origin of Species* in 1859. Were he alive now, Sir Winston would be aware that the "strong arms of science" are attempting to *crush* Christianity. However, the likes of professors Richard Dawkins and Steve Jones, and other atheistic propagandists like Jonathan Miller, are really prophets of pseudo-science. Evolutionary theory – more religious than rational – is founded on fanciful speculation rather than empirical verification. As the popular creation scientist Ken Ham says, evolution is "The Lie": an unscientific fiction, so potent through tiresome repetition that many believe it.

This is the falsehood which inspires modern atheistic secularism, powerfully challenged by best-selling Christian author John Blanchard whose *tour de force* explains why "God does not believe in atheists". During Sir Winston's early years, Darwinism was the dynamic behind late British Imperialist racism, and would later inspire Communism and Fascism alike. Sadly, by that time, Christianity had been weakened by liberal scholarship. Thus, it ceased to offer a persuasive alternative to these destructive ideologies. By now, secularism having largely robbed us of our Christian ethos, we lack the fire of true faith with which to oppose Islam's false faith.

Regarding the scale and impact of Islamic terrorism, there can be no doubt that the Prime Minister was deeply shaken by the events of 7/7 and 7/21. Stating at a press conference that the rules had changed in favour of more stringent security-arrangements, he was not slow to identify the bombers' ideology as "evil". One wonders whether his private thoughts about Islam have changed in the last year; or whether he remains a victim of the kind of widespread deception British Muslims constantly deploy against the gullible public, as illustrated in the tragic killing of Ken Bigley.

After arriving in Baghdad to promote Mr Bigley's release, one of the UK Muslim leaders Dr Hussein said he believed in "the power of prayer" Is this authentic Islam? or were his words simply an attempt to hijack Christian language in order to deceive viewers about Islam's true character? If Muslims believe in the power of prayer, why is

Islamic history red with the power of the sword? – the glaring reality is that "militant" Muhammad's piety was very different from the seemingly "moderate" Muslim cleric's. Indeed, providing a charter for today's terrorists and suicide bombers, the Prophet declared in the *Hadith* (as cited in Gibbon's *Decline and Fall of the Roman Empire*, ed. D. M. Low, 1960, p. 679):

> The sword is the key of heaven and hell: a drop of blood shed in the cause of God, a night in arms, is of more avail than two months of fasting or prayer: whoever falls in battle, his sins are forgiven: at the day of judgement his wounds shall be resplendent as vermilion, and fragrant as musk; and the loss of his limbs shall be supplied by the wings of angels and cherubim.

In his double reference to Islam at the 2004 Labour Party Conference, the Prime Minister distinguished between militants and moderates, insisting that the former represent a "perversion" of Islam. Did Muhammad therefore "pervert" his own teaching? – if not, Mr Blair is guilty of misleading the nation concerning Islam, as he misled us concerning the war in Iraq.

While he argues that the causes of recent UK terrorism predate the Iraq war, Mr Blair cannot deny that the now disastrous and discredited Bush/Blair policy at least aggravated the situation, giving Muslim militants the excuses they need to hit back; so the question remains, "What is the *ultimate* cause of Islamic terrorism if not Islam itself?"

Mr Blair needs to take history lessons from the former Spanish Prime Minister, José María Aznar, whose party was swept from power after 3/11. Aware of the history of al-Andalus (the Moorish occupation of Spain), Mr Aznar traces Islamic violence to its source. "There are those who think that the Madrid attacks are related to the support given by the Spanish government to the Iraq war", he said in a speech in Washington, DC, last year. "The problem with al-Qaeda came from before that – *as long ago as 1,300 years*" (*The Economist*, 30 July 2005, p. 38).

Exactly so! An ex-Muslim Iranian Christian told me that Osama bin Laden represents the purest expression of original Islam. In that Mr

Blair affirmed the Government's intention to introduce so-called "religious hate" legislation at the 2004 conference, does this mean that attempts to correct his own and the so-called Muslim moderates' misinformation will become a criminal offence?

Accordingly, I wrote to the Home Secretary:

> In view of the religious-hate legislation proposed by your predecessor, I beg you to reconsider this highly contentious and problematic policy. Among other things, it will prove utterly unworkable. Apart from inhibiting freedom of speech, it is a recipe for unjust discrimination. While many of us suspect that the entire policy is intended to safeguard Muslim sensitivities, Muslims themselves will not be exempt from accusation if the proposed legislation operates equitably.

> It seems that, while Islamic beliefs are to be protected, Christian beliefs are to remain open to ridicule by all and sundry [eg, the Springer Opera]. However, the fact is, that *The Qur'an* itself is highly hostile to both Judaism and Christianity. Indeed, it arguably qualifies as religious hate-literature. A single specimen makes this clear:

>> 'The Jews say Ezra is the son of Allah, while the Christians say the Messiah is the son of Allah. Such are their assertions, by which they imitate the infidels of old. Allah confound them! How perverse they are! It is He Who has sent forth His apostle with guidance and the true faith to make it triumphant over all religions, however much the idolaters may dislike it' (*Sura* 9: 30 -3).

> Therefore, if Muslims are themselves to avoid prosecution by others, I beg that you discontinue attempts to introduce the proposed legislation. It will only occasion religious and civil strife. If the Islamic community refuses to modernize by allowing open and mature discussion of religious ideas, including their own, without an unrestrained sense of outrage, they must expect similar complaints from the very faith-communities they constantly threaten in their literature.

It is no wonder that the Islamic community has requested that *The Qur'an* be exempt from prosecution. Neither was it a surprise that Charles Clarke was intent on pursuing his predecessor's policy over "religious-hate" legislation. In Norwich, we had no doubts about his secular and multi-faith sympathies. Four years ago, on 16 February 2001, with our assistant pastor, Stephen Quinton, I attended a public meeting for city church leaders with the two Norwich MP's (the other being Dr Ian Gibson).

Invited to submit questions to the MP's, I asked: "In view of the on-going persecution of Christians in Muslim countries, does the UK Government intend to ask Islamic governments to grant the same tolerance and freedom to their Christian minorities as is currently expected and enjoyed by Muslims here in the UK?"

The answer was simple: "The Government has no such policy". Neither MP had any apparent qualms of conscience over the injustice of their stance. In view of the current Test-Match series in Pakistan, should English players be there while Pakistani Christians are suffering for their faith at the hands of Muslims?

This was not to be my last encounter with the two Norwich MP's over Islam. When the Norwich *Evening News* gave extensive and prolonged coverage to my views on Islam in August and September 2004, Dr Gibson told me to "shut up". Attending Charles Clarke's surgery on 8 October, Stephen Quinton was told by the MP that he "deplored" my August press statements about Islam. He did at least indicate that the form of my protest did not amount to an infringement of the legislative proposals currently being considered by the Government.

Thus, earlier calls for my prosecution came to nothing, and I remain undaunted and unphased by the city's double-barrelled political "big shots"! In an attempt to inform Mr Clarke about the nature of the Islamic threat, I sent him copies of all my Islamic documents. In a covering letter, I indicated that he was misinformed if he saw the Muslim community in the UK as a perpetual benign presence. In a brief reply, he concluded that we must "agree to differ" on the issue.

Rather puzzled by this seeming sympathy for Islam, all was explained when I read Anthony Browne's article "This sinister brotherhood – The Left's love affair with the Muslim Association of Britain hides a frightening agenda" (*The Times*, August 11 2004). This unholy political pact was confirmed by Mike O'Brien's shameless admission that Labour must win back the Muslim vote it lost over Iraq (*Daily Mail*, 8 January 2005).

3
ANALYSIS

Whatever secularists or other religious commentators say about Islam, I am utterly persuaded that radical authentic Christianity alone provides the best basis for scrutinizing and assessing it. Because Islam's barbaric ideology is driven by a corrupt theology, non-theological criteria will never enable us to challenge its claims effectively.

However unwelcome some might find the discipline, we must get beyond cultural, historical, social and political criticism – we must go to the heart, and "get theological"; which involves recognizing that Islam's loveless and anti-Christian creed is to be attributed to seven grave defects.

Chief among them is its blasphemous Unitarian denial of the Deity of our Lord Jesus Christ, relegating Him to a mere prophet, inferior to Muhammad.

Second, among the Ninety-nine names for Allah, "God is love" is not one of them. Thus, Muslims shout of Allah's greatness; but they do not sing of his love.

Third, the claim that "Allah is compassionate and merciful" teaches that he is fickle in excusing sin rather than justly forgiving penitents on the basis of a substitutionary atonement (as in Christianity). A case in point is the permission Allah gave to Muhammad to renege on his promise to his wife, Hafsa, not to associate sexually with a Coptic slave after she found him with her (see *The Qur'an, Sura 66: 1-6*).

Fourth, unlike the Judeo/Christian Scriptures in which the rigorous demands of Law are met by a generous provision of Grace, *The Qur'an* is all Law. Hence, Islamic life is driven by a fierce and joyless legalism.

Fifth, the vicious violence intrinsic to Islamic jihad is not an aberration. Unlike Christ's repudiation of faith-propagating violence – "My

17

kingdom is not of this world. If my kingdom were of this world, then would my servants fight" (*John 18: 36*), – Muhammad urges his followers to kill the enemies of Allah – "Slay the idolaters wherever you find them" (*Sura 9: 5*). While medieval Catholic violence: eg, the Crusades: was a *lapse* from Christ's methods, and thus condemned by the New Testament, Islamic violence is in perfect accord with Muhammad's hostile directives [see *Appendix 1*].

Sixth, concerning the character of *The Qur'an* itself, it cannot begin to compare with the contents and integrity of *The Holy Bible*. In view of its Jewish, sub-Christian and pagan sources, what is good in it is not original, and what is original is not good. For every nice verse, there are a hundred nasty ones.

Last, the Muslim case in favour of *The Qur'an* – that the documents of our New Testament are a corrupted version of an earlier original text of the Word of God [supposedly containing references to Muhammed] – collapses with their inability to produce such a text. Indeed, would God have allowed His Word to be lost without trace?

While the BBC lavishly entertains an increasingly decadent nation with the corrupt saga of ancient Rome, its secular anti-Christian agenda driving revisionist history, Islam's conspirators continue to stockpile their terrorist powder-kegs in the cellars of this country's tolerant culture – with little or no protest from Roman Catholic, Anglican, ecumenical and multi-faith leaders.

"Islamic Awareness" events are helping the Muslim community to ingratiate themselves with the rest of us. If their efforts in Oxford this week are anything like the Norwich event in May this year, we need to be on our guard. The University of East Anglia paper, *Concrete*, carried a full-page promotion (*Concrete*, Wednesday, May 18, 2005); so I wrote to the editor as follows:

> As a Christian minister in Norwich, I am gravely concerned at the deceptive and misleading information you published about Islam (*Concrete*, May 18). If the UEA Islam Society is trying to create a "new perception" of Islam, will its members distance themselves

from the intolerance and violence clearly sanctioned by *The Qur'an*, and reinforced in the *Hadith* against Jews, Christians and others?

The intention to "forge a culture of tolerance in a world that is quick to judge" is welcome. However, such a democratic attitude is not consistent with Muhammad's teaching. Indeed, the Saudi Ambassador made it clear last year that democracy and Islam do not mix. [If politics is the art of the possible, Islam cannot co-exist with liberal democratic institutions].

Furthermore, what about religious freedom? – a basic feature of Western democracy? Are Muslims free to embrace a different religion if that is their choice? The answer is "No". I am in receipt of a letter from an ex-Muslim lady who lives in secrecy here in the UK for fear of her life. The subjugation of women is another unwelcome feature of Islam, clearly and unambiguously taught in *The Qur'an*.

Lastly, does the UEA Islam Society intend to urge Islamic governments to grant freedom to Christians? – the very freedom that Muslims expect here in the UK? I ask this in view of almost-daily reports of Christians being butchered for their faith by Muslims.

You will clearly see that my objections to Islam are not the ill-informed "quick-to-judge" response identified in your article. Indeed, I make other very serious criticisms of Islam on our church website (www.geocities.com/nrchurch). Till the UEA Society and others face up to these criticisms, they cannot be surprised if the "old perception" of Islam persists. The question is: Can Islam really alter its image without repudiating the Qu'ranic basis of all it stands for?

The fact is undeniable that Islam's global jihadists – some quietly, others violently – are plotting the overthrow of all we have known for centuries. They are preparing for "UKistan" in no uncertain terms! Tragically, our secularist Government – which Islam aims to subjugate and replace in any case – is playing dangerous games by ignorantly distinguishing between militant and moderate Islam.

The only difference between moderates and militants is between those who keep their mouths shut, and those who don't! The Government and other secularists are deluded by the deceptive mantra "Islam means peace" (reinforced by the early, pre-abbrogated *Sura 2: 256*, and the frequently misquoted *Sura 5: 23*).

But it means nothing of the kind! The Arabic word for "peace" is "Salam", the Hebrew equivalent being "Shalom". No – "Islam" means "Submission": submission to Allah. The only sense in which the *Pax Islama* could mean "peace" is when the tribute-paying enemies of Islam are silenced by conquest, and reduced to a state of *dhimminitude*, or "second class" citizenship. To use Sir Iqbal Sacranie's deceptive expression properly (used to shield Islam from its critics after 7/7) – "*The Qur'an*" is perfectly clear: – it states:

> Make war on them: . . . Fight those who believe not in Allah . . . nor acknowledge the religion of Truth (even if they are of the People of the Book), till they pay the *jizyah* with submission, and are utterly subdued (*Sura 9: 14, 29*).

The Government's failed multicultural programme is driven by Islamic appeasement; not least, on economic grounds. After all, the Abortion Act of 1967 – which continues to sanction "womb murder" on a diabolical scale while murderers are allowed to live – has robbed the nation of five million tax payers, so that Islamic immigrants are judged necessary despite the potentially nation-threatening religion they espouse.

Is the Government reluctant to question Islam because more than 20% of London is already owned by Arab interests? Should we not be concerned at the power of petro-pounds? – not least, when our oil payments are effectively funding the building of mosques in the UK?

Of course, some theorists are vainly advocating a reformation of Islam. However, attempts to pacify and democratize this religion are doomed to failure. It could never happen without a radical rejection of Muhammad's vicious dictates, and a severe abridgement of the ingrained hatred and oppression of *The Qur'an*. The execution and alienation of reformists by Muslim purists in Islamic states surely destroys all hope of such reformation.

So, what is to be done? First, we must be clear what is *not* to be done. Racist attacks must not be encouraged. Non-violent Muslims need protecting as much as anyone else. While Muslim terrorists must be pursued with military rigour, peaceable Muslims must never be persecuted.

Furthermore, speaking as one who loves the Muslim *people*, but not their *religion*, Muslims need rescuing from Islam! That said, unless our immigration policy takes account of the constant potential for jihadic violence provided by *The Qur'an*, and the even more horrific *Hadith*, there is no way of guaranteeing civil order indefinitely. Therefore, if Enoch Powell's dreadful "rivers of blood" prophecy is to be averted in the UK, several things must be implemented. In reverse order of importance, there must be combined political and religious measures, as follows:

1. Reliable information must be made available to community, educational, church and political leaders about authentic Islam. The loveless concept of Allah; the incoherence of *The Qur'an*; Islam's appeal to the baser instincts of human nature; the degradation of women involving female circumcision and forced marriages; honour killings; its bloody jihadism, and a fallaciously -promised erotic paradise for suicide bombers (murderers not martyrs) – all these features must not be hidden.

In responding to the growing threat, our lame Government is failing to face reality. The distinction between moderate and militant Islam misses the point that *the religion itself is the source of the problem*. Indeed, no other religion on earth can claim to match the violence of the Islamic agenda. Seemingly-benign Muslim communities will always be breeding grounds from which their more militant members can recruit jihadists.

2. With active and sensitive compassion, Christians must use all proper means to evangelize Muslims. In the process, there must be no concessions to liberal as well as Muslim denials of the Deity and

grace of Jesus Christ, the Son of God and only Saviour of the world. In short, the case for the pure, life-transforming faith of biblical Christianity must be courageously made. On the religious-education level, the RE component of the National Curriculum must "put the record straight". Teachers must stop pretending that Jesus and Muhammad are on a par, and that *The Holy Bible* and *The Holy Qur'an* teach similarly-positive values.

Without denying that, too often, Christians have failed to demonstrate the compassionate virtues of their Founder, the true character of Muhammad's programme and its devastating dictates must not be hidden from our children. Yes, the Christian Gospel forbids and condemns hatred and violence. The same cannot be said of the message of Muhammad. The children of UK schools must learn the difference between the mercy of the Sermon on the Mount, and the hatred of the *Hadith*. The children of Muslim citizens also must be exposed to the purity of Christ, and not the poison of Muhammad.

3. Compulsory citizenship ceremonies must require Muslims publicly and explicitly to repudiate the jihadic teachings of their religion in perpetuity. Only then may they enjoy the benefits of our open democratic society. ID cards requiring carriers to disavow violence in the pursuit of their agenda must be introduced. If they refuse to do so, or – as is more likely – are convicted of lying on the basis of *taqiyya* [permitted deception] when they sign, they must be deported to countries where the intolerable is tolerated: eg, Saudi Arabia, or back to Pakistan. State benefits should be withdrawn from anyone who, in ultimately working the system to destroy it, refuses to abide by these reasonable, charitable and enlightened democratic ideals. How idiotic can a Government be to allow enemies *of* the State to live *off* the State?

4. Clearly, to reverse the collapse of Christian conviction in our country, nothing less than a reformation of the churches is necessary. The major problem is the preponderance of apostate clergy, many of whom pursue feminist-orientated, New Age gnostic nonsense. These liberal lying prophets of multi-faith ecumenism have robbed us of the faith-foundations of our national heritage.

Trendy clergy and pluralistic post-modern academics are the curse of contemporary Christianity. They are praised for expressing doubts about Christ's Virgin Birth and Resurrection, and applauded for extolling the spurious virtues of Muhammad – and they get paid for their impiety! Recalling the '80's liberal icon, the former Bishop of Durham, Dr David Jenkins, whose rampages through Christological orthodoxy delighted Muslims, a cartoon said it all. The caption beneath a mitred infidel holding his crozier was "Which is the crook?"

While the horrors of Beslan prompted the Archbishop of Canterbury, Dr Rowan Williams, to confess to a "flicker of doubt" in the goodness of God, he failed to express doubts about the Islamic faith. In stating that Muslims might be saved without becoming Christians, he has betrayed Christ.

Looking to the Vatican for guidance will also disappoint us. Notwithstanding the historic and successful Catholic opposition to the Turks at Vienna in 1683, the *Catechism of the Catholic Church* (#841) clearly expresses an accommodation with Islam. The late Pope John Paul II expressed a desire for coöperation between the two faiths. Cardinal Cormac Murphy O'Connor has publicly referred to Islamists as "our Muslim brothers".

Speaking as a Reformed pastor in the Protestant Dissenting tradition (honouring Her Majesty The Queen in her *civil* but not her *religious* rôle), only a return to the authentic Christian, Apostolic, Reformed and Evangelical Faith (as expressed in the Protestant Confessions, the Ten Commandments, the Apostles' Creed, and the Lord's Prayer) will sweep away the shame and stupidity of Political Correctness.

This is the Faith that gave Great Britain its true greatness – and betrayals of this heritage by the liberal religious and educational establishments must be opposed with vigour. With such spirituality, we shall regain our sanity. Of course, such a proposal will irritate rather than inspire the Government. The former Home Secretary's draconian attitude is well known. Sadly, in his ignorance and prejudice, David

Blunkett failed to distinguish between Muslims and Evangelicals. It remains to be seen whether the Government will be successful with its highly contentious and misinformed "religious hatred" Bill.

UPDATE NOTE:
Thankfully, the House of Commons voted against the Government's version of the Racial and Religious Hatred Bill on 31 January 2006. Two votes took place. In the first, the question was whether the racial hatred laws would be changed, and the Government was defeated by ten votes. On the religious hatred issue, the Government was defeated by just one vote. The Prime Minister was present for the first vote but left the House before the second. His absence effectively ensured victory for those opposing Government policy. While it would be better for the new Bill to be removed from the statute book, the final version - reflecting amendments in the House of Lords - contains so many safeguards and protections that it will represent a minimal threat to those who question and criticise Islam. The Government's defeat allays almost all the fears that have been talked about in recent months. It remains a possibility, of course, that the new legal provision could be both abused and altered at a future date. While there is no room for complacency, Christians will recognise in these recent developments a clear instance of Almighty God's merciful providence.

4
PROGNOSIS

In conclusion, I am well aware that this statement will be greeted with howls of derision and outbursts of anger from those whose cherished philosophies I have challenged. They enjoy the freedom to dissent from what I've said. I am no more inclined to oppress them than I am to persecute Muslims. However, if they scorn or simply ignore my solution, a British Islamic regime would never allow them the luxury of dissent if ever its Nazi-like objectives were realized.

If ancient Rome was destroyed from within by its own corruption, and, in the post-Empire era, the UK is fast losing its moral cohesion for similar reasons, there must be national repentance. It is worth noting that church historians of yesteryear viewed the rise of Islam as a Divine judgement on the corruption and decadence of seventh-century Eastern Christianity. Indeed, one may argue that the rapid rise of Islam in "Christian" Europe within the last thirty years or so (see Anthony Browne's report, *The Times*, July 26 2005) – an ominous reality hinted at by Churchill – is to be viewed similarly.

It is sobering to reflect that Turkey was once a flourishing Christian region before Islam swept over it. The tragedy is, that, while many people rightly resent the oppressive prohibitions and barbaric penalties that Islamic shar'iah law would impose (see *The Qur'an, Sura 5: 33*), they reject more holy yet humane Christian values in favour of the immoral life-style which Islam justly laments in Western culture.

Are we surprised when Muslims are not impressed by our fornicating, binge-drinking, drug-taking, foul-mouthed yobbish youth, and the media entertainment which helps to inspire them? Is this what it means to be British? – freedom to be filthy? We should be ashamed of ourselves: children and parents, people and politicians, one and all. Secularism has produced a cesspit society! It is time to repent! And appropriate repentance must go deeper than what the ethical barbarities of Islam might produce.

Indeed, there is an older precedent for the terrible consequences of national apostasy, and the necessity of such repentance. The Old Testament prophet Daniel has much to teach us. If ever a nation suffered from a total culture-quake, it was the Jewish people during the Babylonian captivity. Uprooted from their God-given land in 587 BC, settled far from Jerusalem and the Temple, they were sustained by faith in God and His gracious promise of eventual restoration.

Living in the final years of the captivity, Daniel's faith, courage and integrity mark him out as an "excellent" statesman and man of God (see *Daniel 6: 3*). His humble and prayerful spirituality make him an example for us today. In his prayer for the people, he identifies himself with the nation that had been punished for its sinful rebellion against God (see *Daniel 9: 4-15*). Rather than adopt the dubious modern practice of apologizing for the sins of others, Daniel shared and acknowledged the nation's guilt: "We have sinned; we have done wickedly" (*v 15*).

Being personally virtuous, he had no reason to apologize and resign because of adulterous indiscretions. He never advocated a "back to basics" policy – only to be found out for an extra-marital affair. No – but he had the humility and sincerity to acknowledge himself as a sinner before God, like the rest of us. In deep, heart-felt repentance, Daniel pleaded with God to have mercy on His people: "O my God, incline Your ear, and hear; open Your eyes, and see our desolations, and the city which is called by Your name; for we do not present our supplications before You because of our righteous deeds, but because of Your great mercies" (*v 18*).

Such is the solid piety represented by former Prime Minister John Major's parliamentary predecessor, Oliver Cromwell. To those who are alarmed at the current moral disintegration of the UK, the Lord Protector's words to the Major Generals in 1656 make stirring reading:

Make it a shame to see men bold in sin and profaneness, and God will bless you. You will be blessing to the Nation. . . . Truly, these things do respect the souls of men, and the spirits – which are the men. The mind is the man. If that be kept pure, a man signifies somewhat; if not, I would fain see what difference there is betwixt him and a beast (*Letters and Speeches*, ed. T. Carlyle (1888), iv. 209).

It will interest you to know that twelve years ago, besides publishing my *True Christian Safe Sex Guide* (which advocates exclusively heterosexual marital propriety), I quoted these words in a letter of complaint to the Huntingdon Health Authority about a disgusting, immoral and appallingly-lurid "safe sex" leaflet they had published. Copies were sent to the Huntingdon Conservative Association and Conservative Central Office. I received a personally-signed two-page reply from John Major, dated 30 November 1993 in which he said: "I note your reference to the words of the illustrious former MP for Huntingdon, Oliver Cromwell, but I do not believe we have lost sight of the virtues he recommended". Whatever might have been true a decade ago, is this the belief of today's Tories? If so, there is hope, both for the Conservative Party and the Nation. If not, the future is too bleak to contemplate, especially if the deception that was "New Labour" from its inception (in "stealing" Conservative economics, it was really "Tory Mk 2") continues.

After the reigns of Belshazzar and Darius, Daniel's prayer was answered when Cyrus the Persian became king. The new king's liberal policy eventually allowed the Jews to return to their land. God's merciful promises were fulfilled. While the parallels might be few, may we not plead with God to restore the power of the Gospel, and the consequent blessings of a harmonious society, here in the UK?

Rather than the political scenario of Daniel's day, many Christians consider that our position is more akin to the early Church threatened by opposition from pagan Rome. Be that as it may, let us be sure to undergird every lawful, God-honouring attempt to revive Christian influence in our nation with Daniel's prayer (*v 19*): "O Lord, hear! O Lord, forgive! O Lord, listen and act!" Apart from Him, there is no hope.

This brings me to the heart of my radical Christian message; a message with political as well as personal implications. The eternal salvation of men and women depends entirely on the Person and work of our Lord Jesus Christ. The world's greatest need is to hear the "good news" about Christ (see *John 3: 16; 20: 31*). The greatest service that Christians can render to their fellow human beings is to declare the unique glory and grace of the only Saviour of the world (see *John 1: 29*).

While one-world religious pluralism gains momentum, the faithful Church of Christ must oppose the gross deception of today's multi-faith madness with courage (see *John 14: 6*). The growing hostility to authentic Bible-based Christianity demands single-focus reliance on God alone, as the motto on US currency ["In God we trust"] surely indicates.

Sadly, in his second inaugural speech, President Bush yielded to PC pressure by giving Christianity and Islam positively comparable status. Rightly stressing the importance of "private character" for "freedom" and "the public interest", the President declared that "edifice of character is built in families, supported by communities with standards, and sustained in our national life by the truths of Sinai, the Sermon on the Mount, the words of *The Qur'an*, and the varied faiths of our people".

Apparently unaware of the President's thinking, and in response to my recent article, "Gunpowder, treason . . . and now Islam", an e-mailer from the USA reported with surprise that "your very own Prince Charles was here last week to admonish President Bush for America's disgraceful lack of respect for Islam and Muslims. . . . If he has read the *The Qur'an*, he is either a closet barbarian, or incapable of comprehending the written word".

After questioning the "brightness" of Prince Charles, my correspondent continued: "I'm glad to know that they haven't locked you up for inciting religious hatred, and I only wish that the members of your government and mine understood Islam as well as we do. It's hard to believe that so many brilliant folks could be so obtuse. I'm afraid that our élitist social engineers are going to destroy Western Civilization if we don't do something fast. I have no desire for the utopia they are hell-bent and determined to foist upon us all, despite overwhelming evidence that it will never succeed. Some people never give up, do they?"

Sadly, as though his pluralistic "Defender of faith" instead of "*the* Faith" stance does not already disqualify His Royal Highness from being future Supreme Governour of the Church of England, I had to agree that The Prince of Wales is utterly misinformed. However, the President doesn't appear much brighter than The Prince, in that he spoke highly of Islam at a recent Ramadan dinner at the White House (*English Churchman*, 18 November 2005).

It is a matter of regret that, in her Christmas message for 2004, Her Majesty The Queen presented such a sanitized profile of Islam. What would Her Majesty think about a brave Christian English lad recently ejected from class at a Wiltshire school – a New Labour madrasa? – with a strong pro-Islamic bias? and all because of the dastardly "crime" of allegedly writing "God Save The Queen" on his exercise book (*Daily Express*, 26 October 2005)?

Then, when a Staffordshire school insisted that all written references to Muhammad in GCSE exams must be accompanied by "peace be upon him" (or else marks will be deducted), a father otherwise willing for his child to learn about Islam was branded "racist" by the headteacher for objecting to this Muslim indoctrination (*English Churchman*, 11 November 2005).

We must ask, "What is driving all this?" The fact is, that, just as Roman Catholics have an ultimate allegiance to The Pope, Muslims have a prior allegiance to the *umma* – the global Nation of Islam! I learned recently (18 November) that, in London – Islamic terrorist capital of Europe, – a new radical website declares Her Majesty as an "enemy of Islam" (primarily, it must be said, because of her Government's misguided invasion of Iraq). While Her Majesty's positive comments about Christianity at the General Synod of the Church of England were welcome, a call for Muslim observers was surely utterly misguided (*Daily Telegraph*, 16 November 2005).

5
CONCLUSION

With a continuing and growing assault on our Christian heritage, never was there a greater need to get to grips with the truth of the Bible text: "No man ever spoke like this man" (*John 7: 46*). Thus, I conclude my paper in sermonic mode:

1. NO MAN EVER SPOKE LIKE JESUS CHRIST
And why? He was no ordinary man. He was perfect and sinless. He is the "God-man"; "God manifest in the flesh" (*1 Timothy 3: 16*); The Eternal "Word made flesh" (*John 1: 14*).

Thus, He spoke words of truth, purity, love, kindness and compassion.

He spoke with divine unction, grace and authority. No one else, before or since, ever spoke like Him. He is Creator, King, and Lord of the Universe.

On the other hand, Muhammad was an ordinary man. He was imperfect and sinful. He spoke words of error, impurity, hate and cruelty.

2. NO MAN EVER LIVED LIKE JESUS CHRIST
His life backed up His words. In lip and life, He was perfectly consistent. He brought blessing, healing, comfort and joy to people. His many miracles confirmed His deity. His tender touch declared the compassion of God. He liberated women from the abusive treatment of selfish men. He rejected violence as a method of spreading His message.

No life has ever been lived to match the life of Jesus Christ. On the other hand, Muhammad's life contradicted many of his more noble sayings. His life is not a good example for "private character". His claims cannot compare with Christ's. Spreading his message by the sword, he brought violence and bloodshed to those who refused to submit to his "Allah". He humiliated women. His tenderness was reserved chiefly for his own sexual indulgence, and his stomach (according to wife, A'isha).

3. NO MAN EVER DIED LIKE JESUS CHRIST
While His life and preaching angered the religious establishment of His day, nothing could justify the hatred directed at Him. He was guilty of no sin. Expressing God's mercy to us hell-deserving sinners, Jesus, Saviour of the world, died for our sins. He died, "the just for the unjust, that He might bring us to God" (*1 Peter 3: 18*). In His agonizing crucifixion, He breathed nothing but love and kindness to His enemies. Such dying! Such love! On the other hand, Muhammad died, burdened by his own guilt. Sadly and tragically, his death did not terminate his cruel conquests. Others perpetuated his vicious legacy.

3. NO MAN EVER BLESSED THE HUMAN RACE LIKE JESUS CHRIST
His impact on history is not just the effect of a perpetuation of His memory. Jesus rose from the dead! He lives! The Gospel is the greatest blessing the world has ever known! It has brought forgiveness, love, joy and peace. Christ has mended broken hearts and lives. He has given hope to those in despair. Through Him, the light of heaven has dispelled the darkness of death. He has liberated individuals and nations. The Gospel has delivered people from ignorance, slavery, poverty and degradation. All that is truly good, noble, pure and beautiful comes from Him (even if apostate believers have corrupted His truth).

Christ's resurrection influence continues still where He is accepted, trusted and served. On the other hand, Muhammad died, to rise no more, except to be judged by Christ when He returns. His tomb is not empty. His legacy is ignorance, cruelty, fear and oppression. The continued influence of his teachings is a threat to all that Christ represents.

In conclusion, the case *for* Christ and *against* Muhammad is compelling in every respect. Assessed by every test that may be devised, there is simply no competition; so let us all respond as did the men in our text! May we all acknowledge, believe, trust, love and surrender to the incomparable Christ. May we all rejoice in Him, and seek to make Him known throughout the world.

I am well aware that many in the secular West desire Christ no more than they desire Muhammad. Therefore, I must warn them. Even if they never suffer from some jihadic atrocity, they will stand before the judgement seat of Christ, when He returns to judge the world in righteousness (see 2 *Corinthians 5: 10*).

While opportunity remains, come to Christ! If you are a Muslim, renounce Muhammad, and come to Christ! Then, everything I have tried to express will become wonderfully and experientially true. For my part, I will never serve The Pope or Muhammad. I serve only our Lord Jesus Christ.

I invite you all to serve Him with me. Amen!

Personal Conference Report

First, I wish to thank all those who prayed for the Oxford Conference. In that the event was uncharted waters for me, I felt the need for God's help and guidance more acutely than usual. Well, I am happy to report that He answered our prayers. Notwithstanding the political context, none of the conference concerns – UK sovereignty, alternatives to the EU, the Euro and the UK economy, the future of Conservatism. and UK Defence policy – was alien to my understanding of the Word of God.

Feeling comfortable with what I heard, I was able to make my own contribution with confidence. The LORD enabled me to remain true to my concern to speak for His glory and the best interests of our Nation. I was comforted to find several Christians present, some of whom I knew. Pastor Roland Burrows of Old Hill e-mailed me the next day with his encouragement:

> A short note to thank you for notifying me of the conference we so very much appreciated today. Your own contribution was, as usual, thoroughly researched, and absolutely to the point. It took courage to speak as you did on such a subject, and faithfulness in

weaving into the whole a clear Gospel presentation and challenge. "Them that honour me, I will honour."

Dr Malcolm McCausland and his wife, Margaret, from Cheadle Hulme attended. Their comments are equally positive:

Just a line to say how pleased we were to meet you in Oxford, and to express our appreciation, not only for your address, but also for your clear answers at "question time". I hope that you were encouraged by the meeting, as we were.

Having received an e-copy of my lecture, Cecil Andrews of "Take Heed Ministries", Northern Ireland, responded thus:

Many thanks for sending the details of your lecture. It is absolutely brilliant, and with your permission I should like [next week] to add it to the "Words of Wisdom" section on our website. Will be praying for you, and for a Godly impact through your presentation tomorrow.

I trust that these reactions will dispel any doubts that I, a Minister of the Gospel, am "going political". The Right Revd Barry Shucksmith, Bishop of the Free Church of England (also present) said: "Having a social conscience is not the same thing as preaching a social gospel". If doubts linger, the reading of this lecture should dispel them. While The Lord Tebbit had to depart promptly after his own lecture, he kindly accepted a copy of mine (delivered immediately after his).

Conference being held in the main lecture theatre at Oxford Brookes University, a good number of people attended from many parts of the UK. Opportunities for conversation proved fruitful. It was good to be able to demonstrate that, in our political concerns, the Gospel is the only true antidote to all our personal and national ills. For my son, Hywel (taking time off from academic duties), a defining point was my statement that over and above every other issue, "the human heart is the chief problem".

Finally, please pray for the Lord's continued blessing on this unique opportunity to present the claims of Christ.

Oxford Outing

While the Oxford visit involved degrees of apprehension, some lighter moments were provided by Hywel, who kindly arranged accommodation for me at his college. On the Lord's Day morning, we worshipped together at St Ebbe's, probably the best evangelical church in the city. Following a good spiritual meal, and a splendid lunch at Christ Church, we began a "heritage tour". Walking via Lincoln College, where we saw the monument to a famous former Fellow, John Wesley, we made for Broad Street, and the site of Latimer and Ridley's martyrdom in 1555. The original location of the stake, now in the middle of the street near Balliol College, is marked by cross-shaped stonework. I stood on this sacred spot. Round the corner in St Giles Street, the large, impressive monument honours Latimer, Ridley *and* Cranmer (martyred, 21 March 1556). With a suitable pause for reflection, we had coffee in the Ashmolean Museum.

Back to the car, we headed north-west out of Oxford towards Blenheim Palace. Viewed from a distance, the impressive column of John Churchill, 1st Duke of Marlborough, stood out in the mid-afternoon sun. Our main destination was Bladon Parish Church, and the grave of Sir Winston Churchill. A wreath paid tribute to a "great leader", now surrounded only by the remains of other family members. Having quoted Sir Winston's views on Islam the day before, quiet graveside reflection aroused a sense of privilege.

A site of ancestral interest, the ruined former nunnery at Godstow between Woodstock and Oxford was next on the list. One-time residence of King Henry II's mistress, Rosamund de Clifford, "Fair Rosamund" was buried here in 1177. Renowned for her extraordinary beauty, she was not without penitential piety. What of the King?

A grave of greater and more edifying significance was found at Headington in north-east Oxford. In the churchyard is the quite-unspectacular memorial to C S Lewis, who needs no introduction. His influence lives on *The Chronicles of Narnia, The Screw-tape Letters, Mere Christianity*, and other literary masterpieces. Recalling my engineering course at RAF Farnborough during the early 1960s, I shall always thank God for the faith-nourishing features of *Mere Christianity*, avidly read during tea breaks! At this graveside, I felt grateful to God.

So ended a fascinating afternoon. After tea, I left Hywel and Oxford for Marian and Norfolk.

Appendix 1

QUR'AN QUOTES

Extracts are taken from *The Koran*, tr. N. J. Dawood (Penguin Classics, 4th revised edition, 1974; reprinted 1986).

Of *The Koran Interpreted* (Oxford World Classics paperback, 1998), the English translator, A. J. Arberry states candidly: 'I have called my version an interpretation' (*p. xii*). However, in his introduction, Baghdad-born N. J. Dawood states that he was careful to avoid 'turning the text into an interpretation rather than a translation' (*p. 11*).

WARNING:

The IPCI edition (*Abdullah Yusuf Ali*) of *The Qur'an* (Islamic Vision, Birmingham, England, 1999) is not a reliable translation. An Arabic specialist (whose name is withheld for security reasons) states that this translation is calculated to deceive. It presents a 'soft' version of Islam for western readers. There are numerous examples of defective translation. Also the extensive notes often contradict the Qur'anic text.

Those who wish to assert that Islam is a tolerant religion, committed to peaceful methods of propagation, should reflect carefully on the following quotations. Unlike their less hostile brethren, it is obvious that militant Muslims are more consistent with their 'holy book'. *While Muslim scholars are quick to contextualise this violent language, they cannot deny that it continues to fuel jihadic violence.* While the justly-condemned violence and persecuting activities of so-called Christians - past and present - are emphatically condemned by the Bible (*see Matthew 5: 43-5; 26: 52; Romans 13: 10; 2 Corinthians 10: 4-5; Ephesians 6: 12*), the *The Qur'an* positively teaches the use of force. The highly contrasting depictions of the character of God in *The Bible* and *The Qur'an* and their consequent impact on personal behaviour are too obvious to miss. It is indeed chilling to note N. J. Dawood's reminder that, apart from the opening verses and a few passages in *The Qur'an*, 'the speaker throughout is God' (*p. 9*):

'Believers, retaliation is decreed for you in bloodshed' (*Sura 2: 178*).

'Fight for the sake of Allah those that fight against you, but do not attack them first. Allah does not love the aggressors. Kill them wherever you find them...if they attack you put them to the sword...Fight against them until idolatry is no more and Allah's religion reigns supreme...If any one attacks you, attack him as he attacked you' (*Sura 2: 190-4*).

'Fight for the cause of Allah' (*Sura 2: 244*).

'Those that deny Our revelations We will burn in Hellfire...As for those that have faith and do good works, We shall admit them to gardens watered by running streams, where, wedded to chaste virgins, they shall abide for ever...the believers who do good works, whether men or women, shall enter the gardens of Paradise' (*Sura 4: 55-7, 124*).

'The true believers fight for the cause of Allah, but the infidels fight for idols. Fight then against the friends of Satan' (*Sura 4: 76*).

'Therefore fight for the cause of Allah' (*Sura 4: 84*).

Allah has given those that fight with their goods and their persons a higher rank than those who stay at home. He has promised all a good reward; but far richer is the recompense of those who fight for Him...' (*Sura 4: 96*).

'Unbelievers are those who declare: 'Allah is the Messiah, the Son of Mary'' (*Sura 5: 17*).

'When the sacred months are over, slay the idolaters wherever you find them. Arrest them, besiege them, and lie in ambush everywhere for them...' (*Sura 9: 5*).

'...make war on the leaders of unbelief...' (*Sura 9: 12*).

'Believers, know that the idolaters are unclean...' (*Sura 9: 28*).

'The Jews say Ezra is the son of Allah, while the Christians say the Messiah is the son of Allah. Such are their assertions, by which they imitate the infidels of old. Allah confound them! How perverse they are! They worship . . . the Messiah the son of Mary, as gods besides Allah; though they were ordered to serve one God only. There is no god but Him. Exalted be He above those whom they deify beside Him! . . . It is He who has sent forth His apostle with guidance and the true faith to make it triumphant over all religions, however much the idolaters may dislike it' (*Sura 9: 30-3*).

'Proclaim a woeful punishment to those that hoard up gold and silver and do not spend it in Allah's cause. The day will surely come when their treasures shall be heated in the fire of Hell,...' (*Sura 9: 35*).

'If you do not fight He will punish you sternly and replace you by other men...' (*Sura 9: 39*).

'Whether unarmed or well-equipped, march on and fight for the cause of Allah, with your wealth and your persons' (*Sura 9: 41*).

'Prophet, make war on the unbelievers and the hypocrites and deal rigorously with them. Hell shall be their home: an evil fate' (*Sura 9: 73*).

'Believers, make war on the infidels who dwell around you...' (*Sura 9: 122*).

The terrible events of September 11 brought the character and claims of Islam into sharp focus. Indeed, as reported in the media, the five-page Arabic document discovered by the FBI in the luggage of the suspected terrorist Mohamed Atta silenced the assertions of those who denied that Islam provided any religious motivation for the attacks on New York and Washington. Besides giving instructions about clothes, knives, wills, IDs and passports, the document gave the suicide bombers inspirational incentives from *The Qur'an*, of the kind listed above:

In the name of Allah, the most merciful, the most compassionate... Remember the battle of the Prophet...against the infidels, as he went on building the Islamic state... Continue to recite the Qur'an... You have to be convinced that those few hours that are left in your life are very few. From there you will begin to live the happy life, the infinite paradise... Be optimistic. The Prophet [Muhammad] was always optimistic. Always remember the verses that you would wish for death before you meet it if you only know what the reward after death will be... You will be entering paradise. You will be entering the happiest life, everlasting life.

Appendix 2

WESLEY ON ISLAM

Throughout his long and effective ministry, John Wesley (1703-91) frequently lamented the damaging impact of nominal Christianity. Truthless, faithless, loveless and lifeless Christians provide the best excuse for others to reject the claims of the Gospel of Jesus Christ. What Paul said of the Jews has often sadly been true of Christians: 'The name of God is blasphemed among the Gentiles because of you' (*Romans 2: 24*). How often have modern Muslims taunted so-called 'western Christians' for the moral decadence of their affluent and immoral lifestyle! This is not a new or exclusively Muslim criticism either. Regarding the corruption of the early Eastern Church just before the 7th century rise of Islam, John Wesley remarked that 'Surely Mahometanism was let loose to reform the Christians!' (*Journal* for 5 August 1754). If God permitted the rise of Islam to bring judgement on corrupt Christian civilization, the current Muslim menace may be viewed in the same way.

Of course, secular prosperity tends to encourage the cancer of religious nominalism and indifference. Christ's parable of the Rich Fool says it all (see *Luke 12: 13-21*). Affluence easily robs believers of spiritual sincerity and vitality, and even morality. But what has been true of Jews and Christians, is also true of Muslims. They too have been seduced and 'softened' by the material comforts available in the West and can be just as charming and cultured - and corrupt - as some nominal Christians. They often distance themselves from the past and present violence of Islam in the same breath as reminding Christians of their equally-violent and crusading past.

However, there is a problem. While the Bible condemns the selfish materialism and persecuting outbursts of Christians (chiefly Roman Catholics but sometimes Protestants too), *The Qur'an* urges physical violence in the name of Allah and the spread of Islam. While western Muslims seem to pose little physical threat to their non-Muslim neighbours, they are not consistent with the profile of a good Muslim according to *The Qur'an*. The terrible truth is that what happened in the USA on September 11, 2001 is fully consistent with Qur'anic teaching. Thus, the nominally Christian West faces two challenges. *First*, the spiritual and moral debilitation of its own decadent and hypocritical Christianity (creating a void which many uninformed and cynical westerners fill with Islam); and *second*, the full and frightful consequences of Islamic revival and progress. Despite the disclaimers of many so-called 'moderate' Muslims following the horror of September 11, John Wesley would remind us today of the true character of Islam. We ignore his words at our peril:

> Ever since the religion of Islam appeared in the world, the espousers of it...have been as wolves and tigers to all other nations, rending and tearing all that fell into their merciless paws, and grinding them with their iron teeth; that numberless cities are raised from the foundation, and only their name remaining; that many countries, which were once as the garden of God, are now a desolate wilderness; and that so many once numerous and powerful nations are vanished from the earth! Such was, and is at this day, the rage, the fury, the revenge, of these destroyers of human kind.

> *The Doctrine of Original Sin*, Works (1841), ix. 205.

> How far and wide has this miserable delusion spread over the face of the earth! Insomuch that [Muslims] are considerably more in number (as six to five) than Christians. And by all accounts, ... these are also, in general, as utter strangers to all true religion as their four-footed brethren; as void of mercy as lions and tigers; as much given up to brutal lusts as bulls or goats: so that they are in truth a disgrace to human nature.

> *The General Spread of the Gospel*, Works (1841), vi. 261.

These facts dictate that the Islamic religion should be fearlessly and fervently opposed. John Wesley's brother Charles even composed a hymn on the subject. Perhaps not one of his best, and long since deleted from Methodist hymn books, a strong case may be made for its revival. Its 'non PC' poetry is refreshingly direct and timelessly true:

For the Mahometans

Sun of unclouded righteousness,
With healing in thy wings arise,
A sad benighted world to bless,
Which now in sin and error lies,
Wrapt in Egyptian night profound;
With chains of hellish darkness bound.

2 The smoke of the infernal cave,
Which half the Christian world o'er-spread,
Disperse, thou heavenly Light, and save
The souls by that Imposter led,
That Arab thief, as Satan bold,
Who quite destroy'd thy Asian fold.

3 O might the blood of sprinkling cry
For those who spurn the sprinkled blood!
Assert thy glorious Deity,
Stretch out thine arm, thou Triune God!
The Unitarian fiend expel,
And chase his doctrine back to hell.

4 Come, Father, Son and Holy Ghost,
Thou Three in One, and One in Three!
Resume thy own, for ages lost,
Finish the dire apostasy;
Thy universal claim maintain,
And Lord of the creation reign!

Charles Wesley
(*Hymns for the People called Methodists* (1874), 443)

We may well surmise what John Wesley would say about the events of September 11, 2001: "I told you so!" Doubtless he would add that unless the spineless and spiritless West truly turns to Christ with head and heart, lip and life, talk and walk, then what has happened elsewhere in the past will happen to us in the 21st century. May the God and Father of our Lord Jesus Christ have mercy upon us!

Of course, a greater judgement than Islam could ever inflict on the world is coming. We await the return of our Lord and Saviour Jesus Christ, who will judge the world in righteousness. Then Muslims, merely nominal Christians and others who have rejected Christ as God, Lord and Saviour will tremble in dread and despair. Still, in this eleventh hour and fifty-ninth minute, mercy is available for everyone - including penitent Muslims, as John Wesley eloquently reminds us:

He willeth not that any should perish, but that all should come to repentance; by repentance, to faith in a bleeding Lord; by faith, to spotless love, to the full image of God renewed in the heart, and producing all holiness of conversation. Can you doubt this, when you remember, the Judge of all is likewise the Saviour of all? Hath he not bought you with his own blood, that ye might not perish, but have everlasting life? O make proof of his mercy, rather than his justice; of his love, rather than the thunder of his power! He is not far from every one of us; and he is now come, not to condemn, but to save the world. He standeth in the midst! Sinner, doth he not now, even now, knock at the door of thy heart? O that thou mayest know, at least in this thy day, the things that belong unto thy peace! O that ye may now give yourselves to Him who gave himself for you, in humble faith, in holy, active, patient love! So shall ye rejoice with exceeding joy in his day, when he cometh in the clouds of heaven.

The Great Assize, Works (1841), v. 173.

Notwithstanding their differences over predestination and election, John Calvin would not dissent from Wesley's appeal:

Behold the Turks [= Muslims], which cast away the grace which was purchased for all the world by Jesus Christ: the Jews do the like, ... (*Sermons on Timothy and Titus*, Banner of Truth facs. 1983, p. 177).

Paul makes grace common to all men, not because it in fact extends to all, but because it is offered to all. Although Christ suffered for the sins of the world, and is offered by the goodness of God without distinction to all men, yet not all receive him (*Comment on Romans 5:18*, Oliver & Boyd, 1960, p. 117).

Appendix 3

ISLAM: A REFORMED RESPONSE

When the violence of Islam is criticised, the usual responses by Muslims and others are: What about the Crusades? Isn't Christian history as bloody as Islamic history? What about Northern Ireland? However, such a simplistic comparison ignores a fundamental difference between the two religions, and evades pertinent truth. While the crusades were a failure on the part of medieval Roman Catholicism to obey the New Testament (see *Matthew 5: 43-5; 26: 52; Luke 9: 56; Romans 13: 10; 2 Corinthians 10: 4-5; Ephesians 6: 12*), Islamic violence is in perfect harmony with the dictates of *The Qur'an* (see *Suras 2: 178, 244; 4: 84, 96; 9: 5, 12, 41, 73, 122*).

So, a 'Christian response' to Islam demands careful definition. In short, by the standard of the Bible, both Islam and the Roman Catholic Church are guilty. Furthermore, Muslims were not the only targets of vatican violence. Jews and Protestants have also been victims. While some early Protestants had difficulty in shaking off the violent and unbiblical legacy of Rome, the Reformed Churches appealed to the Bible against both Islamic and Roman persecution. Of all Rome's protestant victims, the Reformed Churches of France suffered the most. From (and even before) the St Bartholomew Massacre (1572) to the Revocation of the Edict of Nantes (1685), the catalogue of crimes against French Reformed believers defies the imagination. Indeed, Rome's methods were hardly different from those of Islam.

The root cause of Rome's policy against the Huguenots was the latter's rejection of papal tyranny and tradition in favour of a pure attachment to biblical doctrine and practice. Thus, the authentic 'Christian response' to both Rome and Islam is the 'Reformed response'. This is clearly reflected in '*The Form and Manner of Baptising Pagans, Jews, Muslims and Anabaptists converted to the Christian Faith; composed by the National Synod of the Reformed Churches of France, assembled at Charenton [near Paris], in the year 1645.*' The form relating to Muslims is worthy of our consideration. It reminds us that the basic issues are those of Scripture, the person and work of Christ and the character of *The Qur'an*:

Q. 1   Do you...believe that the Scriptures of the Old and New Testaments be inspired of God, and contain His whole counsel for the salvation of men, and are the only perfect rule of faith and life?

A. Yes.

Q. 2   Do you...believe that Jesus the son of the blessed virgin Mary, who was conceived in her by the virtue of the Holy Ghost, and formed as to the flesh out of her own substance, is God and man, blessed for evermore, perfect God, and perfect man; man born of a woman in due fulness of time, and God begotten of the Father from everlasting?

A. Yes.

Q. 3   Do you...believe that the Lord Jesus, from his first conception after the flesh, was holy, innocent, without blemish, and separate from sinners; and that he did not suffer death for his own sins, but for ours only?

A. Yes.

Q. 4   Do you...believe that his death is the propitiation for our sins, yea, and for the sins of the whole world; and that this propitiation is infinitely meritorious, through which everlasting glory and salvation were purchased for us?

A. Yes.

Q. 5   Do you...believe that Muhammad was an impostor, and that his *Qur'an* is a sacrilegious heap of idle fancies, full of absurdities, broached on design to set up a false and abominable religion

A. Yes.

Q. 6 Do you...believe that the Gospel of our Lord Jesus Christ is the power of God unto salvation, to everyone that believeth; and that in the Christian religion, only God the Father hath revealed his good will and pleasure for the salvation of men, until the end of the world; and that since its revelation, there is not any new religion to be expected, for that the Lord Jesus Christ is the only great Prophet promised unto the faithful of the Old Testament; and that God having formerly spoken at sundry times, and in divers manners unto men, before the Law, and under the Law, hath spoken to the Church of the New Testament, by the mouth of his only Son the Lord Jesus?

A. Yes.

Q. 7 Give an account of your creed.

A. I believe in God, the Father Almighty, creator of, &c.

Source: John Quick, *Synodicon in Gallia Reformata* (London, 1692), ii. 449.

So may the Huguenots enable us to assess correctly the religious dimension of the current world crisis. While guilty terrorists must be brought to justice, may we avoid a coalition crusade against innocent Muslims. May they only be targeted with truth and lured by love. May God in His infinite grace and mercy bring Muslims and inconsistent Christians to a true confession and expression of the Gospel of His dearly-beloved and only-begotten Son, our Lord Jesus Christ. Only then will the world know peace and harmony.

AMYRAUT ON ISLAM

The famous French Reformed [Huguenot] theologian Moïse Amyraut (1596-1664) provided a forceful critique of Muhammad and Islam. The following extracts are taken from his *Traitté des religions contre ceux qui les estiment toutes indifferentes* (Saumur, 1631):

Tis true, [Muhammad] teaches not only one supreme, but one single and solitary Deity, infinite in essence and power; and condemns all those trifling Deities, which rendered the Pagan Religion so contemptible. He acknowledges that this Deity governs the world by his Providence, and that all is subject to his Empire. He preaches in general that God is a rewarder of virtue, and that he will repay wickedness with suitable punishments. He extols the mercy of God, and declares that he invites men to repentance. He exhorts to good works, and asserts the resurrection with a final judgement of all men at the condemnation of the World. But all these things which are so specious and plausible in themselves, are but as sugar blended with his poisonous doctrines to make them swallowed more pleasingly and inadvertedly; nor needs there any long discourse to discover his imposture.

Two things alone keep up credit among his fellows the falsities which he vented with so outrageous an impudence; force of arms, the terror of which he diffused wheresoever he came, and the profound ignorance of the people that follow him, to whom it is forbidden to enter into any examination of the verity of things. But if he be fouly inconsistent and discordant in the relation of histories, he is no less in the doctrines which he teaches. For the Gospel exhorts universally to patience, and would not have any maintain or advance it otherwise than by sufferings; and though in other things it condemns not wars justly engaged in by Princes for the conservation of their rights and the peace of their dominions, yet in matters of Religion it recommends only constancy in sufferings of the cross, and would have us be contented with that promise, that all shall be so well ordered by the Providence of God, that none shall have cause to complain that He leaves his own in oblivion.

But what does Muhammad in his case? There is not a chapter in all his book, wherein he does not preach fire and sword, wars and massacres for the advancement of his law. He promises rewards in paradise to those that shall acquit themselves valiantly therein, and denounces eternal pain to cowards. And although (as he contradicts himself very frequently) he says sometimes that no person ought to be constrained by force to receive his law, yet himself was the first that began so to make it be believed, and gave special commandments for it, which also has hitherto been practised by his successors upon all occasions.

English translation: *A Treatise Concerning Religions, in Refutation of the Opinion which accounts all indifferent, wherein is also evinced the necessity of a Particular Revelation, And the Verity and preeminence of the Christian Religion above the Pagan, Mahometan, and Jewish rationally Demonstrated* (London, 1660), pp. 343, 350-1.

Appendix 4

CHRIST AND THE TRINITY

Islamic hostility to the Christian doctrines of the Holy Trinity and the Deity of Jesus Christ is an issue of fundamental importance. Popular Muslim literature does not hesitate to oppose these Christian truths (see Dr Naji I. Al-Arfaj, *Just One Message*, 2001, and I. A. Ibrahim (ed.), *A Brief Illustrated Guide to Understanding Islam*, 1996), pp. 45-6, 57-9).

CHRIST IN THE BIBLE AND THE QUR'AN

In Islamic countries, Christian missionaries remind Muslims that *The Qur'an* has a lot to say about Jesus. This fact, so it is argued, is an effective starting point in presenting the Christian Faith to them. However, the same tactic is used by Muslim 'missionaries' in the West to demonstrate how close the two religions really are. "We also believe in Jesus," they say. Thus modern multi-faith gurus argue that 'Jesus' or 'Isa' provides the basis for reconciliation between the two monotheistic faiths.

While it is true that the *The Qur'an* refers to Christ's virgin birth, life, teaching, miracles, death, resurrection, ascension and second coming, the 'Qur'anic Christ' is very different from the 'Biblical Christ'. At this point, Muslims argue that both Jews and the early Christians - 'the People of the Book' - changed or 'twisted' their original documents which, they say, taught the same truth found later in the *The Qur'an* (see *Sura 3: 78-81*). Thus Christians are accused of making invalid claims for Christ's divinity and trinitarian status not found in their original Scriptures. However, this foundational feature of Muslim anti-Christianity is a completely muddled allegation.

First, no Muslim scholar has ever produced a single copy of a supposedly genuine original MS of the Christian Scriptures different from the oldest extant MSS of the New Testament (c. 350 AD). To illustrate: if (skilfully wielding a black marker pen) a prankish schoolboy added glasses and a moustache to a print of the 'Mona Lisa', claiming it was authentic, sceptics could easily prove it to be otherwise by appealing to the original! *Second*, if the original scriptures had been revealed by God, would He have allowed them to be lost or destroyed? *Third*, even the Qur'anic evidence presupposes that at the time of Muhammad (7th century AD), Jews and Christians still possessed their Bibles - the true Torah and the true Gospel (see *Sura 7: 156-7*). The latter are really charged not with having corrupted their MSS but with 'forgetting', 'hiding' and 'doubting' them (see *Suras 42: 13-14; 5: 14-16*). The only valid conclusion is that, at worst, Christians of Muhammad's acquaintance had misrepresented their own copies of the Bible, a view for which evidence certainly exists.

QUR'ANIC CONFUSION ABOUT CHRIST

Turning to *The Qur'an's* testimony to Christ, absolute Muslim hostility to soundly-documented Christian teaching is very evident. The following selection demonstrates the unbridgeable chasm between the 'Biblical Jesus' and the 'Qur'anic Jesus':

'People of the book, do not transgress the bounds of your religion. Speak nothing but the truth about Allah. The Messiah, Jesus the son of Mary, was no more than Allah's apostle and His Word which He conveyed to Mary: a spirit from Him. So believe in Allah and His apostles and do not say: 'Three.' Forbear, and it shall be better for you. Allah is but one God. Allah forbid that He should have a son!' (*Sura 4: 171*).

'The Messiah, the son of Mary, was no more than an apostle' (*Sura 5: 75*).

'Unbelievers are those that say: 'Allah is the Messiah, the Son of Mary.' For the Messiah himself said: 'Children of Israel, serve Allah, my Lord and your Lord.' ... Unbelievers are those that say: 'Allah is one of three.' There is but one God. If they do not desist from so saying, those of them that disbelieve shall be sternly punished' (*Sura 5: 72-3*).

'Then Allah will say: 'Jesus, son of Mary, did you ever say to mankind: "Worship me and my mother as gods beside Allah?" '

(*Sura 5: 116*).

'... the Christians say the Messiah is the son of Allah. Such are their assertions, by which they imitate the infidels of old. Allah confound them! How perverse they are! They worship ... the Messiah the son of Mary, as gods besides Allah; though they were ordered to serve one God only. There is no god but Him. Exalted be He above those whom they deify beside Him! ... It is He who has sent forth His apostle with guidance and the true faith to make it triumphant over all religions, however much the idolaters may dislike it' (*Sura 9: 30-3*).

Thus starry-eyed multi-faith ecumenists can only pursue their delusion by betraying historic Christian teaching. That said, further muddle in Muslim polemic requires comment since there is some truth in *The Qur'an's* anti-trinitarian denunciations. However, it actually tilts at a man of straw. Whether or not he knew of it, the 'trinity' Muhammad scorned was not the orthodox teaching of the Nicene Creed (325 AD) but the bizarre teaching of a 'Christianised' pagan sect known as the Mariamists.

Treating Mary like a goddess, this cult taught a trinity of 'God, Mary and Jesus'. Such is not the teaching of Bible-believing Christians. In this respect, we would agree with Muhammad's stance (see especially *Sura 5: 116* above). That said, judging by The *Qur'an's* clear denial of Christ's deity, there is no reason to believe that Muhammad would have been sympathetic to Nicene orthodoxy.

TRINITARIAN TRUTH

Regarding the person of Christ, Christian orthodoxy rightly affirms the consistency between the virginal conception of Christ and His inclusion within the divine Trinity of Father, Son and Holy Spirit. While an impeccable theological and logical case may be made for the doctrine of the Trinity, it fundamentally depends on the truth of the incarnation, a miraculous phenomenon which transcends logic. Since *The Qur'an* is emphatic in teaching the virgin birth without logic, why can Muslims not accept the orthodox Trinity without logic? And if they affirm the divine nature of the physical conception of Christ, why can they not affirm the divine as well as human nature of the person thus conceived?

Whatever he learned from the Mariamists, some of Muhammad's own language tends to confirm the truth of the very Christian Scriptures he dismissed (see *Sura 4: 171* quoted above). While the Mariamists did 'transgress the bounds' dictated by 'the Book' where Mary was concerned, they arguably did not transgress where Jesus was concerned. Significantly, some of Muhammad's statements about Jesus are in harmony with the Bible without his realising their true significance. Indeed Jesus was an 'apostle' (*Hebrews 3: 1*). He was also the divine 'Word made flesh' (*John 1: 1, 14*). He is also a 'Spirit from God' (see *Galatians 4: 6*).

However, several of the above Qur'anic expressions are meaningless apart from the truth of Christ's deity. *First*, He was an apostle sent by the Father, sharing the Father's nature: 'This is my beloved Son, in whom I am well pleased. Hear Him' (*Matthew 17: 5*). *Second*, as 'the Word made flesh', Jesus visibly expressed the Father's nature: 'No one has seen God at any time. The only-begotten Son, who is in the bosom of the Father, He has declared Him' (*John 1: 18*). *Third*, having an existence prior to His incarnation, Christ had an eternal spiritual identity in which He shared the Father's nature, a fact reflected in the biblical expression 'only-begotten'.

The 'sonship' of Jesus thus relates not to His birth through Mary but to an *eternal* generation in which He thus partook of all the features or attributes of God's eternal being. Mary was merely the vehicle of His human birth at a point in *time*, through whom the *eternal* Son of God derived His *temporal* humanity. Besides viewing Mary as a goddess, the Mariamist heresy arguably implied a physical union between Allah and Mary, against which Muhammad rightly reacted. Over-reacting to such an idea, His horror at the thought of 'Allah having a son' arose from his failure to see the metaphorical form of the legitimate biblical language involved.

THE LIMITS OF LANGUAGE
Since God is not a physical being (see *John 4: 24*), the idea of 'begetting' or 'procreation' invokes an analogy of limited significance only. Indeed, the details of physical procreation have no parallel in the use of the analogy between human and divine 'begetting'; analogy does not mean identity. In short, *a point that Muslims and others miss, the*

biblical 'father–son' terminology *is metaphorical and not literal.* Otherwise, 'God the Father' would have required a 'wife'. The significant parallel is that just as human beings reproduce themselves *according to their own kind*, so, *according to His own kind*, 'God the Father' revealed Himself in Jesus 'God the Son'. The Qur'anic prohibition 'do not say: 'Three.' ... Allah is but one God' exhibits confused and ill-informed thinking. Muslims are right to reject the Mariamist trinity of 'Allah, Mary and Jesus' but wrong to reject the authentic Christian Trinity of 'Father, Son and Holy Spirit'.

Yes, as Jews and Christians both believe, God is but one God. However, His identity is not to be limited to the notion of the single personality of a human individual. Reflecting the plurality of the Hebrew *Elohim*, the name 'God' refers to a being of *one* nature expressed in *three* distinct though perfectly co-ordinated personalities. The identity of a single, common *nature* forbids the conclusion that there are three gods, just as a human 'father, son and grandson' *forbids* the conclusion that three such distinct individuals involve *more than one type of humanness.* In short, in both cases, they are 'three persons with one nature'.

Besides Old Testament anticipations of the doctrine of the Trinity (see *Genesis 1: 26-7; Psalm 2: 7; Isaiah 9: 6*), the fact remains that the Christian Scriptures abound in 'trinitarian' testimony, notwithstanding the absence of the later technical term 'trinity' in the documents themselves (see *Matthew 3: 16-17; 28: 19; John 15: 26; 2 Corinthians 13: 14; Ephesians 1: 3-13; 1 Peter 1: 2; 1 John 5: 7. NB:* While this last text is not found in the some Greek MSS, it is present in the Old Italic versions (Latin translation from Greek, c.150 AD) which predate the oldest extant Greek MSS).

If Muhammad is quoting a verbatim Mariamist statement when he said "Unbelievers are those that say: 'Allah is the Messiah,' " their confusion contributed to his own over-reactionary confusion. While 'God is the Messiah' hardly represents Christian orthodoxy, 'the Messiah is God' certainly does. In Christian terms, the former could be seen to confuse 'Father' and 'Son', whereas the latter simply asserts that the divine Messiah possesses the same divine nature as the Father. Such a distinction of persons within the Godhead is evident in the New Testament, e. g. *John*

14: 8-10; Hebrews 1: 3. An illustration helps elucidate the last mentioned. The Messiah 'being the brightness of [the Father's] glory and the express image of His person' reminds one of an image on a TV screen. While the source of the original visual image is at the point of transmission, the image on the screen is distinct from the transmitted source even though its own visual features are identical with those of the source. Thus Jesus could say, "He who has seen me has seen the Father" (*John 14: 9*).

He clarified this truth in His response to Jewish critics who accused Him of violating the Sabbath (see *John 5: 16-23*). In His reply, Jesus highlights a neglected truth to demonstrate His deity. While the basis for our Sabbath rest is God's 'resting' from His creative activity (see *Genesis 2: 2; Hebrews 4: 4*), He does not require 'rest' as we do. Indeed, we suffer from fatigue in a way God does not (see *Isaiah 40: 28-31*). In this respect, God is constantly 'at work' in sustaining His creation, in providence and in mercy. Thus Jesus stated that 'My Father has been working until now,...'(*v. 17*). In other words, God never stops working!

Let us then note the profound addition that Jesus makes, '... and I have been working.' In other words, Jesus' healing act on the Sabbath reflected not only a just concern with mercy but a divine activity! In claiming the same 'working' status as His father, Jesus made an extraordinary affirmation.

GOD OF GOD

This profound utterance (*v. 17*) produced additional hatred for Christ. In the eyes of His critics, working on the Sabbath and claiming God was His Father merited double condemnation. He was now guilty of blasphemy! Clearly, His critics saw instantly the real significance of what He was saying. Christ was 'making himself equal with God' (*v. 18*). Augustine rightly observed: 'The Jews understood what the Arians would not understand.' The same applies to Muslims, JWs and Liberals today! As our Lord's teaching made continuing and increasing impact, the charge became more specific: 'You being a man, make yourself God' (*John 10: 33*).

This is why the early Trinitarians confessed the truth about Christ in the way they did. He is 'God of God, Light of Light, very God of very God;

begotten, not created, being of one nature with the Father, by whom all things were made' (*The Nicene Creed*, AD 325). The divine nature is therefore truly expressed in the personality of Jesus Christ. He is the 'true offspring' of the eternal God. In Him we see God the Father from whom His divine nature was directly derived in eternity past.

Regarding Christ's deity, several verses indicate that Christ is God (assuming you are using a Byzantine Greek text-based English translation of the Bible, see also 1 Timothy 3: 16). When Thomas called Jesus 'my Lord and my God' (*John 20: 28*), Jesus would have rebuked Thomas for idolatry if He was not 'God'.

Four other important verses are: 'Christ, ... who is over all, the eternally blessed God' (*Romans 9: 5*); 'Our great God and Saviour Jesus Christ' (*Titus 2: 13*); 'But to the Son he says: "Your throne, O God, is forever and ever; ..." ' (*Hebrews 1: 8*) and 'we are in him who is true, in his Son Jesus Christ. He is the true God and eternal life' (*1 John 5: 20*).

In Philippians 2: 9-11, Paul indirectly quotes Isaiah 45: 23 to prove that Jesus is entitled to 'the name which is above every name'. In view of the fact that the Prophet is speaking of 'God', what is the name Paul has in mind? The name is the Hebrew YHWH (*Jahweh* = Greek *kyrios* = LORD, v. 11). Hence I always say to Jehovah's Witnesses that I am 'thrice a JW' believing in 'Jehovah the Father, Jehovah the Son and Jehovah the Holy Spirit'!

While it is true that numerous references distinguish 'God' from 'Jesus' (e. g. *John 17: 3; 1 Corinthians 8: 6; 2 Corinthians 13: 14*), yet the association of their persons implicitly affirms that 'Jesus' shares the honours belonging to the Father. For instance, if 'John' was out walking with his father, and a person wished to identify his father, someone might say to the person, "That's the man and that's his son." Would 'John' be any less a 'man' because he is the 'son' but not the 'father'? Just supposing 'John' was named after his father, it is equally true to say he is 'the son of John' and 'John the son'. He shares his Father's nature and name. That is why it is theologically correct to call Jesus 'God the Son'. This is the glorious truth revealed in John 5: 16-23.

TRINITARIAN ANALOGIES

While not absolutely necessary, analogies can help to clarify the concept of 'trinity'.

As an artist's personality is detected in his paintings, and a composer's in his music, so God reveals Himself in His works. Thus we find analogies of God's triune nature in His creation. Despite their limitations, these analogies help at least to remove rational contempt for the very idea of 'one-in-three-ness'.

1. Cosmic reality possesses the three integral features of space, matter and time:

i. Space has three (and only three) dimensions - length, breadth and height.

ii. Matter has three forms - solid, liquid and gas. No others are possible, e.g. water, ice and steam are distinct forms of 'H_2O'.

iii. Time is past, present and future. No other conceptions exist.

2. Since man is made in the image of God, something of 'God's triune' character may be discerned in human personality: our souls consist of mind, heart, and will within one unified personality.

3. Just as there is one race of mankind but many individual human beings, so the one divine nature is shared by a plurality of persons in the Godhead. 'Many in one' is not hard to comprehend.

4. A father, a son and a grandson are three persons sharing the same human nature. They are all equally human but distinct individuals. Thus Christ is called the 'only begotten Son' of 'God the Father'.

OTHER ANALOGIES

1. The old 3d piece? This was one coin, equivalent in value to three 1d copper coins.

2. The shamrock was Patrick's famous illustration. Each leaf has three

distinct sections, each part sharing the same cell structure.

3. A triangle is one unified shape with three distinct angles (and sides).

4. The 'Trio' chocolate bar is a useful picture of the Trinity. Each of the three sections share the same constituents.

QUR'ANIC CONTRADICTION OVER CHRIST'S CRUCIFIXION
Next to its denials of Christ's deity, *The Qur'an* is self-contradictory over His death. For instance, two statements predict his crucifixion while a third denies it ever happened:

> [The Jews] plotted, and Allah plotted. Allah is the supreme Plotter. He said: 'Jesus, I am about to cause you to die and lift you up to Me. I shall take you away from the unbelievers and exalt your followers above them till the Day of Resurrection' (*Sura 3: 45-55*).

> [Mary] made a sign to [her people], pointing to the child. But they replied: 'How can we speak with a babe in the cradle?' 'Whereupon he spoke and said: 'I am the servant of Allah. He has given me the Gospel and ordained me a prophet. ... He has exhorted me to honour my mother and has purged me of vanity and wickedness. I was blessed on the day I was born, and blessed I shall be on the day of my death; and may peace be upon me on the day when I shall be raised to life' (*Sura 19: 29-35*).

> '[The People of the Book] denied the truth and uttered a monstrous falsehood against Mary. They declared: 'We have put to death the Messiah Jesus the son of Mary, the apostle of Allah.' They did not kill him, nor did they crucify him, but they thought they did. Those that disagreed about him were in doubt concerning his death, for what they knew about it was sheer conjecture; they were not sure that they had slain him. Allah lifted him up to His presence; He is mighty and wise. There is none among the People of the Book but will believe in him before his death; and on the Day of Resurrection he will be a witness against them' (*Sura 4: 156-9*).

Significantly, Islam has no conception of personal forgiveness based on an atonement where the demands of justice and mercy are equally met. Unlike Christians, Muslims have no Saviour in whom their tortured consciences may find forgiveness and peace. Lacking the motive and experience of Christ's love, Muslims cannot enjoy forgiving and being forgiven.

MUSLIMS AND MARY

Despite its anti-Mariamist stance, *The Qur'an* arguably retains too much of the kind of thinking that produced the excessive Mariamist adulation of Mary in the first place, even casting doubt on the original purity of Christ. Indeed, the above quotation (*Sura 19: 29-35*) suggests that Jesus underwent some early process of purification from 'vanity and wickedness'. On the other hand, Mary is described as 'pure' and 'saintly' in a manner alien to the New Testament (see *Suras: 3: 43; 5: 75*).

While the New Testament speaks of Mary as 'highly favoured' and 'blessed', she is not described as sinlessly 'pure'. On the contrary, in her 'Magnificat', she herself implicitly acknowledges that she is sinful and thus in need of 'God my Saviour' (*Luke 1: 47*). In short, her 'saintliness' depended on the same 'grace of God' enjoyed by all Christian believers, not on some innate perfection, far less on a fallacious process of 'canonisation'. Furthermore, her defects are not hidden in the Gospels. When 'about His heavenly Father,s business', did Mary not momentarily forget that Joseph wasn't his father (*Luke 2: 48-9*)? Did 'the Word made flesh' not gently but firmly rebuke Mary's presumption at the wedding at Cana (*John 2: 3-4*)? Did she not by her penitent response (*v. 5*) teach the Church in all ages to bow exclusively to Christ's authority?

The Qur'an's view of Mary *vis-à-vis* Jesus mirrors the same tendency evident in the medieval Roman Catholic Church which produced the very kind of idolisation of Mary (culminating in the immaculate conception dogma of 1854) rightly rejected by the Reformed Church and Islam alike.

Appendix 5

CHRIST AND MUHAMMAD COMPARED

Some otherwise useful Christian books on Muslim outreach discourage the idea of criticising Muhammad. However, when Christ warned against 'false prophets', He provided criteria by which to identify them (see *Matthew 7: 15-20*). Accordingly, it is quite extraordinary that anyone should ever place Jesus and Muhammad in the same kind of category. Writers and educators are guilty of gross deception in failing to distinguish the two 'leaders'. Dr Philip Schaff provides an accurate brief assessment of Muhammad in a portrait that is hardly flattering:

> He was a better man in the period of his adversity and persecution at Mecca, than during his prosperity and triumph at Medina. History records many examples of characters rising from poverty and obscurity to greatness, and then decaying under the sunshine of wealth and power. He degenerated, like Solomon, but did not repent, like the preacher of 'vanity of vanities'. He had a melancholic and nervous temperament, liable to fantastic hallucinations and alternations of high excitement and deep depression, bordering at times on despair and suicide. ... Towards his enemies he was cruel and revengeful. ...
>
> Sir William Muir concedes his original honesty and zeal as a reformer and warner, but assumes a gradual deterioration to the judicial blindness of a self-deceived heart, and even a kind of Satanic inspiration in the later revelations. ... He did not shrink from perfidy. He believed in the use of the sword as the best missionary, and was utterly unscrupulous as to the means of success. He could take pleasure in cruel and perfidious assassination, could gloat over the massacre of entire tribes, and savagely consign the innocent babe to the fires of hell. ... Muhammad was a slave of sensual passion. Aisha [his favourite wife], who knew him best in his private character and habits, used

to say: "The prophet loved three things, women, perfumes and food; he had his heart's desire of the first two, but not of the last."

The motives of his excess in polygamy were his sensuality which grew with his years, and his desire for male offspring. His followers excused or justified him [because of] the difficulties of his prophetic office, which were so great that God gave him a compensation in sexual enjoyment, and endowed him with greater capacity than thirty ordinary men. ... He had at least fourteen legal wives, and a number of slave concubines besides. At his death he left nine widows. He claimed special revelations which gave him greater liberty of sexual indulgence than ordinary Muslims (who are restricted to four wives), and exempted him from the prohibition of marrying near relatives. ... He married [Aisha] when she was a girl of nine years [which makes him a paedophile in modern terms]. ... To compare such a man with Jesus is preposterous and even blasphemous. Jesus was the sinless Saviour of sinners; Mohammed was a sinner, and he knew and confessed it. He falls far below Moses or Elijah, or any of the prophets in moral purity (see *History of the Christian Church* (1883), iv. 143-203).

Appendix 6

THE CARTOON COMMOTION
Free speech or Christian speech?

'Let your speech always be with grace, seasoned with salt,
that you may know how you ought to answer each one'
(*Colossians 4: 6*).

'Great is my boldness of speech towards you, ...'
(2 *Corinthians 7: 4*).

My initial response to the Danish cartoon commotion (*February 2006*) was to deplore the idiocy of 'free speech' secularists. Was this not an 'own goal' of such stupidity, needlessly to anger the Muslim world by mocking Muhammad? I further thought, while 'free speech' should promote healthy debate through robust argument, must that involve insulting language or images? I certainly concluded that insult and ridicule are not tools a Christian communicator may use.

Christians do not relish the opportunity to say absolutely anything, without any constraints. Truth and holiness place definite limits on what may or may not be uttered. Yes, engage in debate, refute point by point, but do not use insult and mockery. Yes, Christian witness must be bold and uncompromising, but it must be 'gracious' in manner and intent, even when 'salty' straight talking is demanded.

What we are seeing is a crisis among secularists. The 'PC' secularists wish to limit free speech to appease the Muslim community. Frustrated by such constraint, 'non PC' secularists wish to express 'Islamophobia', their 'lunatic fringe' media cartoonists grabbing the worst headlines imaginable. It has also exposed the hypocrisy of the 'PC' secularists. For instance, Foreign Secretary Jack Straw has voiced his disapproval of the cartoons but has he said anything about the insulting and offensive Jerry Springer Opera? Double standards, surely!

While too many 'official' Christians have been intimidated by the 'PC' agenda, genuine vocal Christians are caught in the middle. Sadly, the offending cartoons have highlighted the Islamic problem in a way that stifled public discussion has failed to do. The scale and blood-thirsty vehemence of the Muslim reaction simply underlines the true nature of the Islamic problem. The simple fact is that while all kinds of Christian vilification leave the truth of Christianity unscathed, there is too much truth behind the cartoons - and the Muslims know it.

So genuine Christians must do two things. *First* they must not be afraid to reveal the truth about Islam. *Second*, they must preach the full and glorious truth of Jesus Christ, for the benefit of Muslims and secularists alike. Instead of Islamic 'hate speech' and secular 'free speech' there must be 'Christian speech'. This is the only way forward.

Those who persist in asserting that Islam is a tolerant religion, committed to peaceful methods of propagation, should look again at *Appendix 1*. They will then see where the likes of the recently-convicted Sheikh Abu Hamza get their inspiration from. Yes, - to repeat myself – there have been so-called Christians who have behaved like butchers. However, unlike their Muslim equivalents, they are condemned by the New Testament. Reader, note how different Christianity is from the religion of Muhammad:

'[Christ said:] "You have heard that it was said, 'You shall love your neighbour and hate your enemy.' But I say to you, love your enemies, bless those who curse you, do good to those who hate you, and pray for those who spitefully use you and persecute you, that you may be sons of your Father in heaven; ..."' (*Matthew 5: 43-5*).

[Paul wrote:] 'For we ourselves were also once foolish, disobedient, deceived, serving various lusts and pleasures, living in malice and envy, hateful and hating one another. But ... the kindness and love of God our Saviour towards man appeared, ... Let the word of Christ dwell in you richly in all wisdom, ... Abhor what is evil. Cling to what is good. Be kindly affectionate to one another with brotherly love, ... Bless those who persecute you; bless and do not curse. Rejoice with those who rejoice, and weep with those who weep. ... Repay no one evil for evil. Have regard for good things in the sight of all men. If it is possible, as much as depends on you, live peaceably with all men' (*Titus 3: 4-5; Colossians 3: 16; Romans 12: 9-18*).

Appendix 7

THE MYTH OF MUSLIM MODERATION

As reported by Melanie Phillips, a recent 'Populus' poll of British Muslims, commissioned by a coalition of Jewish community groups (www.timesonline.co.uk), produced some alarming findings for Britain's Jews: Nearly two fifths (37%) believe that the Jewish community in Britain is a legitimate target 'as part of the ongoing struggle for justice in the Middle East'. Moreover, only 52 per cent think that the state of Israel has the right to exist, with 30 per cent disagreeing, a big minority. One in six of all Muslims questioned thinks suicide bombings can sometimes be justified in Israel, though many fewer (7 per cent) say the same about Britain. This is broadly comparable to the number justifying suicide attacks in ICM and YouGov polls of British Muslims after the July 7 attacks...12 per cent of 18 to 24-year-old Muslims believe that suicide bombings can be justified here, and 21 per cent in Israel. A 20% of all Muslims, and 25% of men, say suicide attacks against the military can be justified, though only 7 per cent say this about civilians.

These are ... horrifying figures which reveal that a huge proportion of British Muslims are not 'moderate'' by any reasonable interpretation of the word. There are officially 1.6 million Muslims and only about 300,000 identifying British Jews. If these findings are accurate - and this was a small poll of 500 Muslims - it would mean that around 600,000 British Muslims believed Britain's 300,000 Jews were a 'legitimate target'.

Note also the reason: the Middle East conflict. So much for those who claim that anti-Zionism and antisemitism are totally distinct. Among the beleaguered 300,000 it doesn't quite feel like that. If there's still any doubt about the inseparability of these two hatreds, other findings of this poll reveal both the horrifying extent and depth of the anti-Jewish prejudice among British Muslims and the extent to which they have swallowed the demented, Nazi-style libels and conspiracy theories which pour unstoppably out of the Muslim world. Nearly half of British Muslims actually believe this stuff. That is a staggering proportion, and a vast problem. But who can be surprised, when it is a stock-in-trade of the Muslim world that the Jews are behind every single bad thing that happens?

As reported by James Hamilton in a recent edition of the 'Sunday Herald' (www.sundayherald.com/54197), a survey finds 40% of Muslims want Sharia law. Four in 10 UK Muslims want hard-line Sharia law introduced in parts of

Britain, according to a new poll. One in five also expressed sympathy with the "feelings and motives" of the July 7 suicide bombers who killed 52 innocent people in London. However, while UK Muslims come over as alienated from mainstream society, 91% said they feel "loyal" to Britain. My question is "why?" Probably because while they enjoy UK material benefits, Muslims know that, in time, given their birth-rate, demographic changes will eventually make it easier to achieve their long-term objectives at the ballot box.

Further reading

R. Atkinson, *Europe's Full Circle* (Compuprint Publishing, 1996)

J. Blanchard, *Does God Believe in Atheists?* (Evangelical Press, 2000)

W. F. Campbell, *The Qur'an and the Bible in the light of history and science* (Arab World Ministries, 1986)

B. M. Chedid, *Islam: what every Christian should know* (Evangelical Press, 2004)

G. Felix, *Quaid-e-Azam' Vision: Christians in Pakistan – The Battle for Justice* (Agape Press, 2001)

A. Hilton, *The Principality and Power of Europe* (Dorchester House Publications, 1997)

P. Hitchens, *The Abolition of Britain* (Quartet Books Limited, 2000)

G. Little, *The Mystery of Islam* (Crown of Life Ministries, Inc, 2003)

B. M. Madany, *The Bible and Islam: sharing God's Word with a Muslim* (Back to God Hour, 1992)

A. Manhattan, *The Vatican's Holocaust* (Ozark Books, 1986)

_____, *The Vatican Billions* (Chick Publications, 1983)

Sir W. Muir, *The Life of Mahomet*, (Smith, Elder, 1877)

E. Paris, *The Vatican Against Europe* (Protestant Truth Society, rep. 1988)

_____, *The Secret History of the Jesuits* (Chick Publications, 1973)

D. Richardson, *Secrets of the Koran* (Regal Books, 2003)

P. Sookhdeo, *Understanding Islamic Terrorism* (Isaac Publishing, 2004)

_____, *Islam in Britain* (Isaac Publishing, 2005)

_____, *A Christian's Pocket Guide to Islam* (Christian Focus & Isaac Publications, 2001)

R. Sookhdeo, *Secrets Behind the Burqa: Islam, Women and the West* (Isaac Publishing, 2004)

M. Steer, *A Christian's Evangelistic Pocket Guide to Islam* (Christian Focus, 2003)

A. Zaka & D. Coleman, *The Truth about Islam* (P&R Publishing, 2004)

S. M. Zwemer, *The Moslem Doctrine of God* (facs. American Tract Society, 1905)

_____, *The Muslim Christ* (facs.Message for Muslims Trust Oliphant,1912)

URGENT AND IMPORTANT.

What will you leave behind for the Children?

Most of us want to pass on something worthwhile to those who succeed us. We invite you to consider two vital questions about the kind of society we shall be leaving for the generation that follows us.

1. The loss of our political freedom

Britain had a unique record of establishing Parliamentary democracy here and abroad, and a reputation for maintaining the freedom of individuals to speak, believe and worship according to their conscience. These achievements, hard-won and defended by the loss of many British lives, are factors which draw so many asylum-seekers here.

The proposed European Constitution would, in effect, transfer power from our elected government to unelected Commissioners in Europe - who are intent on imposing control over every aspect our individual lives. They would sweep away the British Constitution and our Common Law, built up from Magna Carta onwards. The most powerful nation in the world today, the United States, was built upon the Christian, Protestant, culture of the British.

2. The moral decline

Our British Constitution demands that, when our monarch is crowned, a Bible is presented to the King or Queen, who then swears on oath to maintain the laws of God, our Creator and Judge.

Britain is a country founded upon the Christian faith. We have grown up with respect for the moral law, as set out in the Ten

Commandments, for the orderly conduct of mankind for all time.

Those of us who are able to compare the general conduct of society today with the accepted standards of conduct forty years ago, will recognise a very serious deterioration, with increased violence, vandalism, broken relationships, dishonesty and selfishness. and undisciplined behaviour. This is very marked in the breakdown in the attitude to marriage and family life, the foundation of a stable society. It is in the family where discipline begins in a loving atmosphere. Discipline is the parents responsibility.

Without that, education becomes difficult for schools, and children are left to experiment with drugs, alcohol and sexual lust. They are easily enticed into physical and spiritual damage for life. Minority pressure groups .have in recent years been influencing our governments to relax laws which had been enacted for the moral security of our social fabric. Such action will only accelerate the breakdown in respect for the law, and lead to demands for further relaxation.

Unless we protect our national independence, and the unique Christian discipline under which Britain flourished and became such a force for good in the world, we shall leave our children with a much less attractive society in which to live. We need to consider as **a matter of urgency** how to reverse the decline of our nation. You may wish to add your name and address and send this leaflet to your local M.P.

Name _____ Address _____

_____

_____

Published June 2004 by: Moral Recovery UK, 66 Chippingfield, HARLOW, Essex, CM17 ODJ. If you are in broad sympathy with the contents of this leaflet, and could help in any way with its wider distribution, please telephone David on: 01763 260461.